Science Biographies

Neil Armstrong

Catherine Chambers

Raintree

Chicago, Illinois

To contact Capstone Global Library please call
800-747-4992, or visit our web site www.capstonepub.com

Edited by Dan Nunn, Adam Miller, and Diyan Leake
Designed by Cynthia Akiyoshi
Picture research by Tracy Cummins
Production by Helen McCreath
Originated by Capstone Global Library Ltd
Printed and bound in China by CTPS

17 16 15 14 13
10 9 8 7 6 5 4 3 2 1

Library of Congress Cataloging-in-Publication Data

Chambers, Catherine, 1954- author.
  Neil Armstrong / Catherine Chambers.
    pages cm.—(Science biographies)
  Summary: "This book traces the life of Neil Armstrong,
from his early childhood and education through his sources
of inspiration and challenges faced, early successes, and the
moon-landing for which he is best known. A timeline at the end
of the book summarizes key milestones and achievements of
Armstrong's life."—Provided by publisher.
  Includes bibliographical references and index.
  ISBN 978-1-4109-6237-9 (hb)—ISBN 978-1-4109-6244-7 (pb)
1. Armstrong, Neil, 1930-2012—Juvenile literature. 2. Project
Apollo (U.S.)—Juvenile literature. 3. Astronauts—United
States—Biography—Juvenile literature. 4. Space flight to the
moon—Juvenile literature. I. Title.
  TL789.85.A75C43 2014
  629.450092—dc23   2013014218

Acknowledgments
We would like to thank the following for permission to
reproduce photographs: Alamy pp. 5 (© interfoto), 9 (© David
McGill), 10 (© BG Motorsports); AP Photo p. 12 (Associated
Press); Corbis pp. 6 (© Corbis), 8 (© David Howells); Getty
Images pp. 18 (Rolls Press/Popperfoto), 24 (Time Life Pictures/
NASA), 28 (Jose Jordan/AFP); istockphoto p. 13 (Jason Titzer);
NASA pp. 4 (Johnson Space Center Media Archive), 19, 20,
21, 22, 23, 25, 26, 27 (Bill Taub), design elements; Courtesy
ot the Ohio Historical Society pp. 7, 17; Shutterstock p. 15
(© DeepGreen); design elements (© Dr_Flash, © Vacclav,
© RoyStudio.eu, © David Woods); U.S. Air Force p. 14; U.S.
Department of Defense p. 11; U.S. Navy p. 16 (Photo by Petty
Officer 3rd Class Travis K. Mendoza).

Cover photograph of Neil Armstrong reproduced with
permission of NASA and of the full Moon reproduced with
permission of Shutterstock (© Dundanim).

Every effort has been made to contact copyright holders
of material reproduced in this book. Any omissions will
be rectified in subsequent printings if notice is given to
the publisher.

All the Internet addresses (URLs) given in this book were valid
at the time of going to press. However, due to the dynamic
nature of the Internet, some addresses may have changed, or
sites may have changed or ceased to exist since publication.
While the author and publisher regret any inconvenience this
may cause readers, no responsibility for any such changes can
be accepted by either the author or the publisher.

Contents

Some words are shown in **bold**, like this. You can find out what they mean by looking in the glossary.

Who Was Neil Armstrong?

Imagine a world where the solar system was just a mystery seen through a telescope, and where the Moon was a ball of blue mountains and valleys. Passenger flights across the Atlantic Ocean were a new thrill. Jet airplanes were only just making their first trails in the skies.

Into this world was born the first man to step out onto the Moon. A man who was also a remarkable pilot, **aerospace** engineer, and astronaut. His name was Neil Alden Armstrong, and he was born on August 5, 1930.

This is Neil Armstrong inside the vehicle that landed on the Moon on July 20, 1969.

Neil started life in the country town of Wapakoneta, Ohio. His parents were Stephen and Viola Armstrong. Neil had a sister, June, and a brother, Dean. Neil got the qualities of "inventiveness, concentration, organization, and perseverance" from his mother. He got his passion for airplanes from his father.

Top technology

Seaplanes that could land on water were developed in the 1930s. Massive rocket-shaped balloons called **zeppelins** took tourists across the seas. But pilots had to wait for new jet technology before they could fly at high **altitudes**.

In Awe of the Airplane

What inspired Neil to take to the air? His father took him to the Cleveland Air Race at the age of just two. Neil also enjoyed playing with a tin toy airplane that his mother bought for him. At the age of six, he went on his first flight, in a Ford Trimotor plane. His brother, Dean, recalled that this was the most important early experience of Neil's life.

The Tin Goose

The Ford Trimotor was built in 1927 as one of the first all-metal planes. It was nicknamed the "Tin Goose." The plane's three engines took it higher and faster than others of the time. In 1929, the Norwegian pilot Berndt Balehen (1899–1973) flew it over the South Pole.

Neil himself said his deep interest in flight grew from the age of eight or nine. He spent hours making model airplanes. More than this, he drew designs never seen before, with retractable landing gear. That is where the wheels pull up under the airplane's belly at takeoff. With this incredible imagination, it is no surprise that Neil wanted to be a designer, not a pilot!

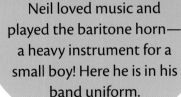

Neil loved music and played the baritone horn— a heavy instrument for a small boy! Here he is in his band uniform.

Up, Up, and Away!

Neil's father was an **auditor** for the state of Ohio. The job meant that he traveled a lot with his family, checking how the state was spending its money. The Armstrongs had to move 20 times!

When Neil was 14, the family returned to Wapakoneta, and Neil settled down well at Blume High School. He joined the Scout movement and was encouraged to explore. This love of exploring his own country and beyond never left him.

Wapakoneta's Armstrong Air & Space Museum displays Neil's flying history.

ARMSTRONG
AIR & SPACE MUSEUM

FIRST FLIGHT

At just 15, Neil and his friends took flying lessons at an airfield in Wapakoneta. The lessons were expensive, so Neil worked in a pharmacy for 40 cents an hour to pay for them. He passed his test on his 16th birthday, and he took his **first solo flight** just a week later!

First aircraft

At Wapakoneta, there were old World War II planes and training craft such as the Vultee BT-13 and the Fairchild PT-19. There was also the new Aeronca Chief training aircraft. Neil flew this basic Aeronca model called Champ (above). The pilot's seat is at the front and raised above a dipped nose, for good visibility.

Designs for the Skies

Neil applied to college to study aerospace engineering, following his true passion. He hoped the U.S. Navy would help pay for his studies. So, at the age of just 16, Neil calmly flew 300 miles (480 kilometers) to register for the U.S. Navy scholarship-qualifying exam!

Neil enrolled at Purdue University in West Lafayette, Indiana, in 1947. He received the Holloway Plan naval scholarship, too. For the plan, Neil had to study for two years, serve three in the U.S. Navy, and study for two more.

Neil joined Purdue Airport's Avionics Club in his spare time. He worked on planes like this 1940s Boeing Stearman PT-17 Kaydet.

A FULL COURSE LOAD

Neil studied some very serious math, together with engineering drawing, **welding**, and the behavior of hot metals. Studying and getting fit through the physical education program filled Neil's days.

Breaking records

On October 14, 1947, Captain Charles "Chuck" Yeager broke the **sound barrier** in the rocket-powered Bell X-1. Neil admired the Bell X-1, but he was sad to see the end of records achieved through older **propeller planes**. His heroes were pioneer pilots such as Charles Lindbergh and Amelia Earhart.

In this photograph, Chuck Yeager is standing by the side of the Bell X-1. He named it *Glamorous Glennis*, after his wife!

GLAMOROUS GLENNIS

War Above the Clouds

In 1949, Armstrong left Purdue for three years to train at Pensacola Naval Air Station in Florida. He gained his Naval Aviator **wings** in 1950. By then, the United States was at war with Korea. But Armstrong did not take part until 1951.

Armstrong often flew alongside his commanding officer, Marshall Beebe. They flew extremely fast F9F-2 Panthers. The days of the slow Aeronca Champ were a happy but distant memory.

The crowds cheered as Armstrong's aircraft carrier returned to the United States in 1952.

No fear of flying

Armstrong survived a close shave while landing his aircraft on the deck of an aircraft carrier. Another time, his plane was hit by enemy gunfire and struck a tall pole. Armstrong had to bail out. Did he rethink flying? Never!

Returning to learning

Armstrong was 22 when he returned to Purdue University. He was confident after his Navy experiences and graduated in 1955. Armstrong became truly content when he became engaged to another Purdue student, Janet Shearon.

Armstrong gained both knowledge and practical experience at Purdue University.

In the Fast Lane

The United States' National Advisory Committee for Aeronautics (NACA) was forging ahead with superfast **jet propulsion**. After leaving Purdue, Armstrong was eager to be a test pilot at NACA's High-Speed Flight Station (H-SFS) at Edwards Air Force Base in California.

Disappointment—then delight

There were no openings at H-SFS, but Armstrong's application was sent to the Lewis Flight Propulsion Laboratory in Cleveland, Ohio. He was hired there!

At Lewis, Armstrong and fellow crew member Joseph Algranti flew this P-82 aircraft. It had a test rocket that was launched from underneath its belly.

At Lewis, Armstrong worked as a scientist and engineer as much as a test pilot. He investigated anti-icing systems and the effects of heat on **supersonic** aircraft. In addition to this, Armstrong designed components, analyzed data, and drew many diagrams. He really got to know supersonic flight and space flight inside out.

The open road

Was Armstrong just a very serious, hardworking man? No, not at all! He loved cars and traveling. In 1952, he bought an Oldsmobile 88, like the one in this picture. He toured from Mexico to Canada with his brother, Dean.

Moving On Up

Armstrong stayed at Lewis for only five months before he got his dream job. He became a test pilot for the NACA High-Speed Flight Station at Edwards Air Force Base. There, Armstrong tested X-15s, aircraft that flew at supersonic speeds way above the speed of sound. He tested the aircrafts' performance and helped thrust forward supersonic and rocket science.

A cloud forms behind this FA-18 Hornet just as it breaks the sound barrier.

Armstrong's work led to a place in the Man in Space Soonest program in 1958. This was the same year that NACA became NASA, the National Aeronautics and Space Administration. The Man in Space Soonest program tested flight equipment for manned space. Armstrong was on his way up!

Armstrong married Janet Shearon in 1956. They had two sons. Their daughter died from cancer when she was only three.

Not all plain sailing

Armstrong's technical knowledge was greatly admired. But some criticized him as a pilot. Chuck Yeager thought he was too mechanical and lacked natural flair. Armstrong did have accidents at Edwards, but so did others. He really pushed limits, which made accidents more likely.

The Chosen Few

The Soviet Union (now Russia) was the first country to send a person into space. Then, on May 25, 1961, U.S. President John F. Kennedy made a promise. By 1970, his country would land a man on the Moon and return him safely to Earth.

On April 12, 1961, the Russian Yuri Gagarin became the first person in space.

At this time, the United States was well into its manned space program, Project Mercury (1959–1963). On May 5, 1961, it launched its first person, Alan Shepard, into space.

What about Armstrong? In 1962, he became one of the "New Nine" astronauts assigned to the Gemini space program. So far, Mercury had launched one person at a time. Gemini aimed to send two. Later, Apollo would send three—and aim for the Moon!

Armstrong had to pass desert survival training before he could go to the Moon.

Tested to the limits

Armstrong had to go through many tests to see if he was fit for space travel and its extreme temperatures. His ears were squirted with ice water and his feet were plunged in it! He sat in heat of 145 degrees Fahrenheit (63 degrees Celsius). But he had fun wearing a spacesuit in the **weightlessness simulator!**

A Spin in Space

Armstrong approached *Agena* very slowly as they docked, at about 3 inches (8 centimeters) per second.

At last! Armstrong was chosen as the **command pilot** on Gemini 8. His copilot was David Scott. Their mission was groundbreaking. They had to **dock**, or link up their spacecraft, with *Agena*, a **module** already in space. Scott was to perform a space walk.

Armstrong was forced to land Gemini 8 three days early. This meant he splashed down in the middle of the Pacific Ocean, instead of the Atlantic Ocean.

A CLOSE SHAVE

On March 16, 1966, they blasted off toward *Agena* and docked successfully. But the two spacecraft began to roll uncontrollably. Fuel was running out. Armstrong cut short the mission and pulled away from *Agena*. Still in a spin, he switched on the **reentry control system**. The spinning stopped! Armstrong prepared for splashdown. Saved! But he was disappointed that David Scott's space walk never happened.

Cool, calm, and commanding

Armstrong had proved his worth. After Gemini 8, he was chosen as backup command pilot for Gemini 11—and then for Apollo 8. Armstrong knew that after backing-up Apollo 8, he would fly Apollo 11—the mission to the Moon! In fact, he was chosen to command it.

Apollo, Here We Come!

Neil Armstrong, Michael Collins, and Buzz Aldrin shot into space on July 16, 1969, from the Kennedy Space Center in Florida. In Houston, Texas, a huge team of space experts kept in contact with the astronauts. Nearly 600 million people watched on live television.

Apollo 11 had the *Saturn V* service module (SM), *Columbia* command module (CM), and *Eagle* lunar module (LM).

SM

CM

LM

UNITED STATES

Perfect partners

Like Armstrong, Michael Collins (born 1930) had been a test pilot at Edwards. He had orbited Earth 44 times on Gemini 10. Buzz Aldrin (born 1930) was also a first-class pilot and space scientist. He flew on Gemini 12 and had spent many hours walking outside the spacecraft.

Collins piloted Apollo 11's *Saturn V* rocket, which launched the astronauts and space modules. It was so fast it seemed a little unstable. But the rocket circled Earth one-and-a-half times, then steered toward the Moon.

Saturn V then fell away, and Collins piloted the *Columbia* module closer to the Moon's surface. Armstrong and Aldrin crawled into *Eagle*, the lunar module. *Eagle* separated from *Columbia*, and on July 20, Armstrong and Aldrin began their Moon landing.

Liftoff! At 9:32 a.m. on July 16, 1969, the *Saturn V* rocket launched Apollo 11.

The First Man on the Moon

Armstrong took *Eagle*'s controls. They were not on target. All Armstrong could see was boulders and clouds of dust. He looked ahead at a smoother spot and made a gentle touchdown.

Armstrong contacted ground control, saying, "Houston! Tranquility Base here. The *Eagle* has landed." For six and a half hours, Armstrong and Aldrin checked out *Eagle* and their moon-walking equipment. It was time to open the hatch.

Splashdown!

"ONE SMALL STEP..."

As he stepped onto the Moon, Armstrong said: "That's one small step for a man, one giant leap for mankind." He took photos, set up a television link, and planted the U.S. flag. Aldrin joined him. They spent two and a half hours taking soil samples and more photos. Then it was time to rejoin *Columbia*.

A real leader

Aldrin said of Armstrong, "He got me there and he got me back. I made a couple of mistakes and fortunately they weren't that crucial!" Armstrong also took the best rock and soil samples of any Moon walker.

25

After Apollo

For three weeks, Armstrong and his team were **quarantined**, or kept away from other people. This was in case they had a space disease!

Armstrong had fun playing the ukulele while in quarantine!

Then, in open-top cars, they paraded through the streets of New York, Chicago, and Los Angeles—all in one day! The team toured 24 countries and 27 cities in 45 days, shaking hands with people all around the world.

Armstrong was a great ambassador, but he found fame hard to handle. The pressure led to the end of his marriage with Janet. In 1994, Armstrong found happiness again when he married Carol Knight.

STILL A BUSY LIFE

Armstrong became NASA's deputy associate administrator and held this position until 1971. For eight years after that, he was professor of aerospace engineering at the University of Cincinnati, in Ohio. He also gave advice to science and technology businesses.

Armstrong loved meeting people, but he soon hated the media spotlight.

Mission complete

Apollo missions to the Moon ended in 1972, after six landings on the Moon. After that, NASA aimed further, even to Mars, where robots, not humans, carry out experiments.

Remembering Armstrong

Even toward the end of his life, Armstrong said he dreamed of flying a manned mission to Mars!

Armstrong had a heart operation on August 7, 2012. Sadly, there were complications following the operation. Armstrong died on August 25.

Armstrong posed at age 75 in front of a photo of his younger self. When Armstrong died, seven years later, President Barack Obama called him a national hero.

"Think of Neil Armstrong"

After his death, Armstrong's family together made this plea: "Honor his example of service, accomplishment, and modesty, and the next time you walk outside on a clear night and see the Moon smiling down at you, think of Neil Armstrong and give him a wink."

Timeline

1930   Neil Alden Armstrong is born in Wapakoneta, Ohio, on August 5

1936   Flies for the first time, in a Ford Trimotor Plane at the Cleveland Air Race

1938   Starts to make model airplanes and airplane designs

1945   Takes flying lessons at the airfield in Wapakoneta

1946   Passes his flying exams and gets his pilot's license at just 16 years old

1947   Enrolls at Purdue University to study aerospace engineering; receives a scholarship from the U.S. Navy

1949   Interrupts his studies to serve three years in the Navy, which is a condition of his scholarship

1950   Gains his Naval Aviator wings

1951   Serves in the Korean War

1952   Returns to Purdue University

1955   Gets his degree; works as a flight scientist and engineer at Lewis Flight Propulsion Laboratory; moves to Edward Air Force Base, where he flies at supersonic speed

1956   Marries Janet Shearon

1958   Is selected for the NASA Man in Space Soonest program to train for space flight; continues to work as a scientist and engineer

1961   The Russian Yuri Gagarin becomes the first person in space. U.S. President John Kennedy promises that the United States will land a man on the Moon before 1970.

1962   Armstrong becomes one of the "New Nine" astronauts on the Gemini manned space program

1966   Armstrong and David Scott pilot the *Gemini 8* mission to dock with a module in space

1969   Armstrong is chosen to command Apollo 11. On July 20, Armstrong, Buzz Aldrin, and Michael Collins reach the Moon, where Armstrong takes the first human step.

1971   Armstrong returns to space science and engineering; leaves NASA and spends the rest of his life as a teacher, researcher, and technology business advisor

2012   Neil Alden Armstrong dies on August 25

Glossary

aerospace Earth's atmosphere and space beyond it

altitude height, especially above Earth

auditor person who examines money accounts

command pilot pilot in charge of a mission

dock link up with another module in space

first solo flight pilot's first flight on his or her own after passing flying exams

jet propulsion jet of gas rushing backward that shoots a rocket or airplane forward

module small pod built for astronauts to fly in or to take equipment into space

propeller plane airplane that moves forward when engines turn propellers

quarantined when a person is shut away from other people to prevent the spread of disease

reentry control system control system designed to help a spacecraft reenter Earth's atmosphere

seaplane airplane with smooth runners that enable it to land on water

sound barrier speed-of-sound point that is difficult for aircraft to pass

supersonic traveling faster than the speed of sound

weightlessness simulator machine made to copy the weightless conditions found in space so that astronauts can practice moving in these conditions

welding joining two pieces of metal by melting their edges and pressing on them to make a solid joint

wings badge gained when a pilot passes a flying test

zeppelin massive gas-filled balloon that flies people in a cabin attached underneath

Find Out More

Books

Edward, Roberta. *Who Was Neil Armstrong?* New York: Grosset and Dunlap, 2012.

Hunter, Nick. *Space* (Explorer Tales). Chicago: Raintree, 2012.

Wilkinson, Philip. *Spacebusters: The Race to the Moon* (DK Readers). New York: Dorling Kindersley, 2012.

Internet sites

Facthound offers a safe, fun way to find Internet sites related to this book. All of the sites on Facthound have been researched by our staff.

Here's all you do:
Visit **www.facthound.com**
Type in this code: 9781410962379

Places to visit

Armstrong Air and Space Museum
500 Apollo Drive
Wapakoneta, Ohio 45895-9780
www.armstrongmuseum.org

National Air and Space Museum
Independence Avenue at 6th Street, SW
Washington, D.C. 20560
airandspace.si.edu

Space Center Houston
1601 NASA Parkway
Houston, Texas 77058
spacecenter.org

Index